A LITTLE BOOK OF
ANIMAL RIDDLES

Jim Murphy

SCHOLASTIC INC.

New York   Toronto   London   Auckland   Sydney

To Barbara

ISBN 0-590-41193-4

Copyright © 1988 by James Murphy.
All rights reserved. Published by Scholastic Inc.
Art direction by Diana Hrisinko
Book design by Theresa Fitzgerald

12 11 10 9 8 7 6 5 4 3 2 1   8 9/8 0 1 2 3/9

Printed in the U.S.A.   08
First Scholastic printing, March 1988

What does an elephant do when he breaks his toe?

He calls a tow truck.

Why do little pigs
eat so much?

They want to make hogs of themselves.

How do you get in touch
with a fish?

Just drop him a line.

What happened when the
monkey saw the banana?

The banana split.

What side of a chicken
has the most feathers?

The outside.

Why did the elephant run
away from the circus?

He was tired of working for peanuts.

Why don't little leopards like
to play hide and seek?

Because they are always spotted.

Why shouldn't you put an
ad in the newspaper if your
dog runs away?

Dogs can't read.

What do hippopotamuses have that
no other animal has?

Baby Hippopotamuses.

Why is it hard to carry on a
conversation with a goat around?

He keeps butting in.

What do they call little
gray cats in California?

Kittens.

What is a twip?

A twip is what a wabbit takes
when he wides on a twain.

Why was the mother owl worried
about her little son?

He just didn't give a hoot.

What do you call an
Eskimo cow?

An Eskimoo.

Why do hummingbirds hum?

They don't know the words.

How do you know when there is
an elephant in your refrigerator?

You can't close the door.

Why don't giraffes eat very much?

They make a little go a long way.

Why do mother kangaroos
hate rainy days?

The kids have to play inside.

Why do cows wear bells?

Their horns don't work.

What is black and white and black
and white and black and white?

A penguin rolling down a snowbank.

What is gray, has big ears and a trunk,
and weighs less than a pound?

A mouse going on vacation.

THE END